You Are in Ancient Greece

Ivan Minnis

www.raintreepublishers.co.uk
Visit our website to find out more information about **Raintree** books.

To order:
☎ Phone 44 (0) 1865 888112
🖷 Send a fax to 44 (0) 1865 314091
💻 Visit the Raintree Bookshop at **www.raintreepublishers.co.uk** to browse our catalogue and order online.

First published in Great Britain by Raintree,
Halley Court, Jordan Hill, Oxford OX2 8EJ,
part of Harcourt Education.
Raintree is a registered trademark of Harcourt
Education Ltd.

Editorial: Nick Hunter and Catherine Clarke
Design: Michelle Lisseter, Richard Parker and
Celia Floyd
Illustrations: Art Construction
Picture Research: Maria Joannou and Ginny
Stroud-Lewis
Production: Kevin Blackman

Originated by Dot Gradations Ltd
Printed and bound in China by South China
Printing Company

ISBN 1 844 43286 6
08 07 06 05 04
10 9 8 7 6 5 4 3 2 1

British Library Cataloguing in Publication Data
Minnis, Ivan
You Are in Ancient Greece. – (You Are There)
938
A full catalogue record for this book is available
from the British Library.

Acknowledgements
The publishers would like to thank the following
for permission to reproduce photographs:
AKG Images pp. **5**, **7** (Erich Lessing), **8** (Erich
Lessing), **11** (Erich Lessing), **13** (Erich Lessing),
14 (Erich Lessing), **17** (Erich Lessing), **19** (Erich
Lessing), **20** (Nimatallah), **21** (Andrea Baguzzi),
23, **26** (Erich Lessing), **28** (Erich Lessing), **29**
(Erich Lessing); Ancient Art and Architecture
pp. **6**, **12** (Ronald Sheridan), **15**, **18** (Ronald
Sheridan), **22** (Ronald Sheridan), **24** (Ronald
Sheridan), **25**, **27** (Dr S. Coyne); Bildarchiv
Preussicher Kuturbesitz p. **16**; Corbis pp. **9**
(The MIT Collection), **10** (Wolfgang Kaehler);
Photodisc p. **4**.

Cover photograph of the Parthenon, reproduced
with permission of Corbis (Larry Lee
Photography).

Every effort has been made to contact copyright
holders of any material reproduced in this book.
Any omissions will be rectified in subsequent
printings if notice is given to the publishers.

The paper used to print this book comes from
sustainable resources.

Contents

Any words appearing in bold, **like this**, are explained
in the Glossary.

The Greek world

There were many great **civilizations** around the world 2500 years ago. In the Middle East, the Hebrews and Persians were building great cities. In north-east Africa, ancient Egypt was the most powerful civilization and in central America, the Mayans were building huge pyramids.

In southern Europe, a civilization was developing in the mountainous land that is now called Greece. Ancient Greek civilization was at its most powerful between 800 and 146 BC, when it was taken over by the Romans.

The sacred Parthenon temple was completed in 432 BC.

Classical Athens

Ancient Greece was made up of many different city-states. Each one ruled itself but they had many things in common. Athens and Sparta were the most powerful states. In this book you will travel back in time to Athens at the time of Pericles. He was the leader of Athens in about 460 BC.

Ancient Greece lies beside the Mediterranean Sea. It is made up of city-states such as Athens and Sparta.

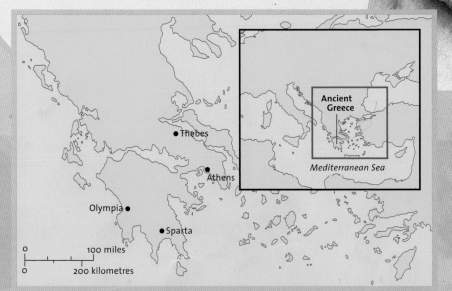

This statue shows the great leader, Pericles.

The ancient Greeks

As you walk through the busy streets of Athens you see rich businessmen and **craftsmen** working in their shops. There are also poor **peasants** and labourers, and many **slaves** who are forced to work hard by their masters.

Everyone wears a **chiton**. This is made from two large pieces of cloth, held together by pins. You pull it over your head and tie it around your waist. Women wear their chitons long, to the ground, while men gather them under their belts so that they only hang to their knees. Children dress in the same way as their parents.

This vase painting shows a slave girl or servant helping her mistress to dress.

Both rich and poor dress in much the same way. Richer people may be able to afford brightly coloured cloths. Most chitons are plain white and made of wool.

In fashion

You may see some people wearing hats called petasus. These protect you from the sun. Tanned skin is very unfashionable. It shows that you have to work hard outdoors, rather than relaxing indoors.

Women grow their hair long and tie it in plaits or ponytails. Men keep their hair short and grow beards, unless they are soldiers.

In this marble statue, the goddess Athena is shown wearing a long, flowing chiton.

A Greek city

Athens is a very beautiful city. There are many important buildings around its busy streets. The best place to go is the **agora**. This is the marketplace in the middle of Athens. People gather here to buy food, cloth and pottery. Others come to watch jugglers entertain the crowd. Near the marketplace is the stoa. This is a building with many shops and stalls, a bit like a shopping centre. It is a good place to meet friends.

City houses

Athens is a busy city with many houses. They are made of mud with red clay roof tiles and are usually two storeys high.

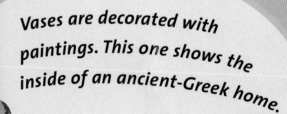

Vases are decorated with paintings. This one shows the inside of an ancient-Greek home.

8

Most houses have two or three rooms built around a small **courtyard**. The family spend a lot of time in the courtyard, eating and relaxing.

You can walk to the Acropolis along the Panathenaic Way, a beautiful path leading from the agora.

Towering above the city is the **Acropolis**. This is where the temples and altars of the goddess Athena are found. She is said to protect the city.

Farming and fishing

Life is very hard for farmers in Greece. The soil is poor and rocky and the **climate** is very hot. On flatter land, the farmers plough their fields to grow wheat or barley. **Slaves** do a lot of the work, but children are also expected to help out. Greek women help out at busy times, but their main job is to manage the household.

Olives, figs and grapes are grown on the poorer soil. Olives are very important. They give oil, which can be used for cooking and to burn in lamps.

You see olive trees on many Greek hillsides.

Goats are kept on the rocky hillsides. They are able to feed amongst the rocks. Their milk can be drunk or made into cheese. Children often watch over the goats, ready to warn the farmers if there is any trouble.

Catching fish

Fishing is also very important. Greece is almost surrounded by the sea. Fishermen travel out to sea in small boats. They catch all kinds of fish to sell at the marketplace.

There are plenty of fish to be caught in ancient Greece. These men are fishing with a rod and net.

Food and drink

When you wake up in the morning you will eat a breakfast of bread soaked in wine. The wine softens the bread, which is often very hard. Both rich and poor eat a lot of bread and everyone drinks wine, even the children. This is because the water is dirty and may make you sick.

Bread is a very important food in ancient Greece. These women are kneading the dough ready for baking.

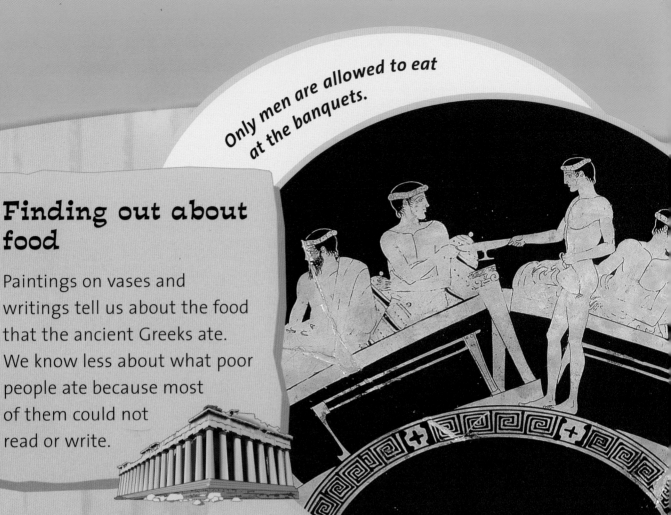

Finding out about food

Paintings on vases and writings tell us about the food that the ancient Greeks ate. We know less about what poor people ate because most of them could not read or write.

Healthy eating

Meat goes off very easily in the hot sun. There are no fridges to keep it fresh. Fish is much more popular. It can be bought fresh from the market. Goats' cheese, olives, figs and vegetables are also eaten. This means that you have a healthy diet, with plenty of vitamins and not too much fat.

Sometimes rich men hold great **banquets** called symposia. During the long meal there are poetry readings, music and games. Women and children are not allowed.

Growing up

When you are very young, you will be expected to help out around the home or work in the fields. If you are a boy, you may start school at the age of seven. Only rich families can afford to send their children to school. At school you learn reading, writing and maths, as well as poetry and music. Most boys stay at school until the age of fourteen. Then they go out to work. Girls do not usually go to school, although some are taught how to read and write at home.

This young man is being taught how to play the lyre by his music teacher.

When children have time to play, they have toys such as wooden dolls, spinning tops and board games.

Growing up in Sparta

Sparta is another city-state in Greece. Its people are very tough. Boys and girls are sent away to **military** school at the age of seven. Boys learn to be tough soldiers. Girls are also made strong and healthy, so that their children will make good soldiers. After leaving school, boys must stay in the army. Even when they are married they live in the barracks away from their wives.

Spartan soldiers are feared by all the other people of Greece.

Reading and writing

At school in Athens boys are taught to read and write. They learn to write on **wax tablets**, scratching out the letters using a **stylus**. This means that if they make any mistakes the wax can be smoothed over and used again. Older boys may be allowed to write on special paper called papyrus. They can use pens and ink.

This boy is learning from his teacher, how to read.

The ancient Greeks are famous for their writings. They do not know it, but their writings will continue to be read by future **civilizations** for thousands of years.

Finding out about writing

We know about Greek writings because people still read them today. Socrates taught that discussing ideas was the best way to learn. Although his works are very famous he wrote none of his thoughts down. His ideas were written down by his pupil, Plato. Herodotus wrote books on important events, such as the wars the Greeks fought. These were the first real history books. We know less about women, because they left fewer writings.

The ancient Greeks admire great thinkers such as Plato.

Science and technology

There are many great scientists and **inventors** in ancient Greece. The ancient Greeks are always trying to understand the world around them. Their **astronomers** study the stars and give them names.

Craftsmen produce many useful things that make people's lives easier. Blacksmiths make armour and weapons for soldiers, and shoes for horses from metal. In the streets of Athens you might see the first fire engine. It pumps water from a wooden box to put out fires. Fires are common because the houses are built so close together.

Ancient-Greek blacksmiths use a hot furnace to help them make lots of different tools.

Finding out about discoveries and inventions

Many of the ideas and inventions of the ancient Greeks are still used. We use the names the Greeks gave to the stars in the sky. The ideas of Hippocrates are still used by doctors. The Greek **mathematician** Pythagoras made many important discoveries that are still taught in schools.

The doctors of ancient Greece are very skilled. This doctor is carefully treating a wound.

Masters of medicine

The Greeks also know a lot about medicine. Greek doctors know that the bark of the willow tree can be used as a painkiller. Hippocrates is the most famous doctor.

Greek art

As you walk around Athens you will notice how beautiful many of the buildings are. Most public buildings have tall columns and wonderful carvings called **friezes**. Climb up the steep hill to the **Acropolis** and you will see amazing friezes on the huge buildings. Temples and public places are decorated with statues of the gods, famous **citizens** and sporting heroes. These statues are carved from blocks of stone by Greek **sculptors**.

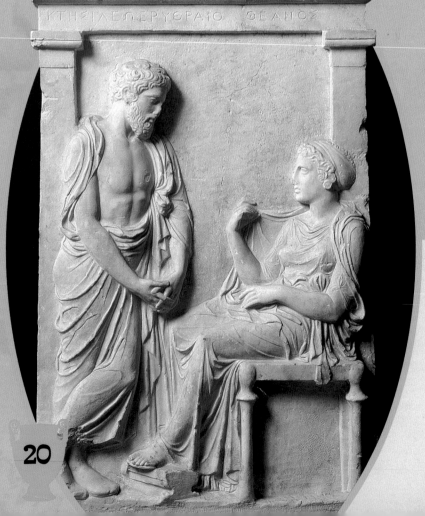

In this beautiful carving, a husband and wife are relaxing at home.

Finding out about art

Paintings on vases tell us how the ancient Greeks lived. Statues can also tell us what they looked like and how they dressed.

Greek pottery

You may also notice how beautiful Greek pottery is. The best is made in Kerameikos, where the potters of Athens work. An artist scratches beautiful pictures on to the soft clay. Some pictures are of **myths** and legends, others are of everyday scenes. The pots are made of reddish clay, which is shaped and then hardened in a hot oven called a kiln.

Skilled potters make beautiful vases such as this one. It shows people dancing.

Entertainment

The people of Athens love going to the theatre. If you are lucky you may be able to see a play in the Dionysus Theatre. It can hold thousands of people. Theatre festivals go on for days, with the audience returning for many shows.

People at this theatre in Epidauros sit on stone steps high above the actors on stage.

stone steps for audience to sit on

stage where actors perform

Watching the show

Your ticket for the theatre costs two obols, but the very poor can get in for free. Everyone sits on stone steps. It might be a good idea to bring a cushion – the steps can get sore after a few shows.

On stage there are two or three actors playing different roles. All of the actors are men. They wear masks to show the different characters and their moods.

Heroes of the Olympic Games are honoured with statues. This is a discus thrower.

Finding out about the Olympic Games

Sporting events were also popular. The most famous of these were the Olympic Games. These were held every four years. Competitors from all over Greece took part. Only men could attend. We know about the games because lots of pictures have been found, as well as the original Olympic Stadium at Olympia.

Greek government

Ancient Greece is not really a country at all – it is made up of many different city-states. They sometimes come together to fight a common enemy, but more often they are at war with each other!

Athens and Sparta

As you travel around ancient Greece you will find that many city-states are ruled in different ways.

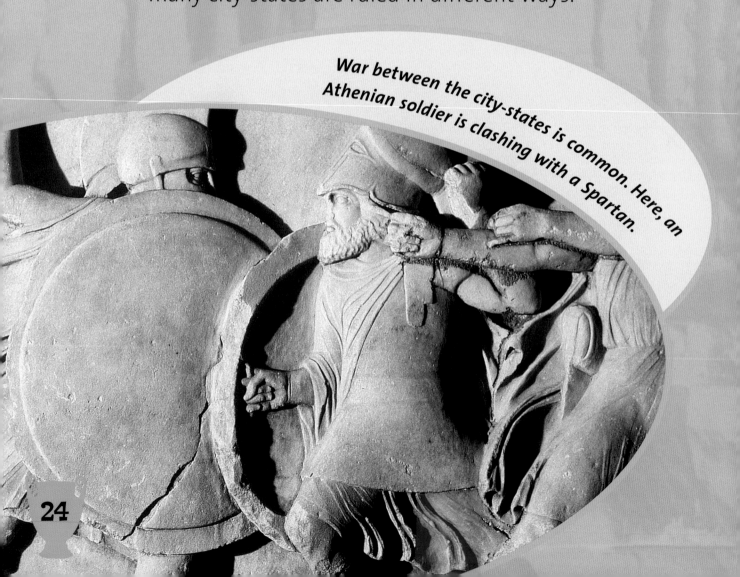

War between the city-states is common. Here, an Athenian soldier is clashing with a Spartan.

Athens is a **democracy**. All of the **citizens** come together to have a say, or **vote**, when there is an important choice to be made. Women, children and **slaves** cannot vote.

Sparta is ruled by the army. Generals make all of the important choices. It is not surprising that they have the strongest army of all the city-states.

Finding out about democracy

Most modern countries are democracies. This means that the people vote for a government to run the country. The word democracy began as a Greek word. It means 'rule by the people'. Athens became the first democracy in 508 BC. Today, we believe that democracy means rule by all adult citizens – not just the men.

The men of Athens drop these ballots into different pots to vote for their leader.

Greek religion

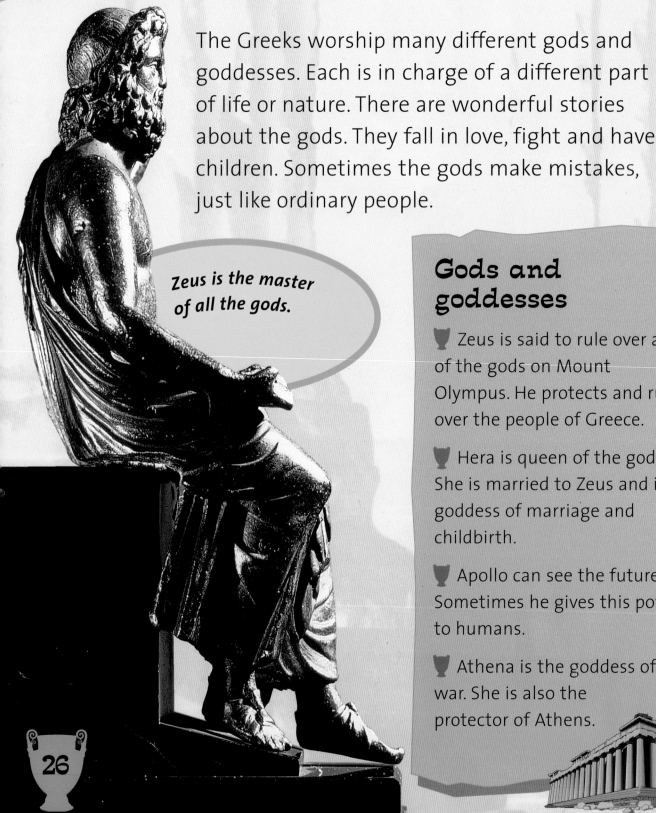

The Greeks worship many different gods and goddesses. Each is in charge of a different part of life or nature. There are wonderful stories about the gods. They fall in love, fight and have children. Sometimes the gods make mistakes, just like ordinary people.

Zeus is the master of all the gods.

Gods and goddesses

🏆 Zeus is said to rule over all of the gods on Mount Olympus. He protects and rules over the people of Greece.

🏆 Hera is queen of the gods. She is married to Zeus and is goddess of marriage and childbirth.

🏆 Apollo can see the future. Sometimes he gives this power to humans.

🏆 Athena is the goddess of war. She is also the protector of Athens.

Games are held at the stadium at Delphi, in honour of the god Apollo.

Each god or goddess has their own temple. These are beautiful buildings where priests offer **sacrifices** to keep the gods happy. Festivals are held throughout the year. Sometimes these include plays and sporting events, like the Olympic Games. All parts of ancient-Greek life, from art to entertainment, are meant to show respect to the gods.

Facts for ancient Greece

Now you know a bit about ancient Greece and its people. Here are a few things you need to know to get by in ancient Greece:

Months of the year

City-states each have their own names for the months of the year. This is the calendar of Athens:

July – *Hecatombaion*

August – *Metageitnion*

September– *Boedromion*

October – *Pyanopsion*

November– *Maimacterion*

December– *Poseideion*

January– *Gamelion*

February – *Anthesterion*

March – *Elaphebolion*

April – *Mounychion*

May - *Thargelion*

June – *Scirophorion*

You will need to know about weights and measures. An ancient-Greek talent is the same as 26 kilograms.

This ancient-Greek coin shows the head of Artemis, the goddess of wild animals and the hunt.

Dates to remember:

around 800 BC: Greece is made up of several small city-states

508 BC: government by **democracy** begins in Athens

447–432 BC: **Parthenon** built in Athens

146 BC: ancient Greece is taken over by the Romans.

Money

The ancient Greeks are some of the earliest people to use money.

Their main coin is the drachma. A skilled builder earns about 1 drachma per day. It is divided into 6 obols.

1 talent is worth 6000 drachmas – this is a huge amount of money.

Find out for yourself

Unfortunately, you cannot travel back in time to ancient Greece, but you can still find out lots about the ancient Greeks and how they lived. You will find the answers to some of your questions in this book. You can also use other books and the Internet.

Books to read

Ancient Greeks (British Museum Activity Book), Jenny Chattingham (British Museum Press, 1999)
History Starts Here: The Ancient Greeks, John Malam (Hodder Wayland, 2003)

Using the Internet

Explore the Internet to find out more about ancient Greece. Websites can change, but if one of the links below no longer works, don't worry. Use a search engine, such as www.yahooligans.com and type in keywords such as 'Athens', '**Acropolis**', 'Olympic Games' and 'ancient Greece'.

Websites

http://www.bbc.co.uk/schools/landmarks/ancientgreece/main_menu.shtml
Take a look at this fun, interactive site.
http://www.historyforkids.org/learn/greeks/index.htm
Lots of facts plus ideas for fun projects.

Disclaimer
All the Internet addresses (URLs) given in this book were valid at the time of going to press. However, due to the dynamic nature of the Internet, some addresses may have changed, or sites may have ceased to exist since publication. While the author and publishers regret any inconvenience this may cause readers, no responsibility for any such changes can be accepted by either the author or the publishers

Glossary

Acropolis   hilltop fortress in ancient Athens

agora   public buildings and shops in the centre of ancient-Greek towns

astronomer   someone who studies the position of the Sun, Moon and stars

banquet   grand meal, with lots of food

chiton   loose, sleeveless robe worn by ancient Greeks

citizen   important man in ancient Greece involved in the running of a town

civilization   united group of people living together

climate   weather conditions over a long period of time

courtyard   walled open space that is part of a building

craftsman   someone who has been specially trained to make something by hand

democracy   country in which the people choose their leaders

frieze   painted or sculpted decorative strip on a wall

inventor   person who makes or discovers something for the first time

mathematician   person who spends time studying numbers

military   to do with armies or soldiers

myth   story used to try and explain nature or events in the past

Parthenon   main temple of the goddess Athena, built at the Acropolis

peasant   poor farmer or farm worker

sacrifice   gift to the gods

sculptor   artist who creates solid carvings from wood or stone for decoration

slave   person held captive and forced to work for a master

stylus   pointed instrument or pen used for writing on wax tablets

vote   make a choice or give your opinion

wax tablet   sheet of wax used for writing on before, or instead of, paper

Index

Titles in the *You Are There* series include:

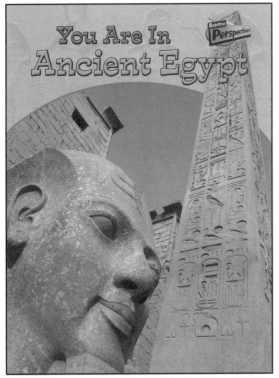

Hardback   1 844 43285 8

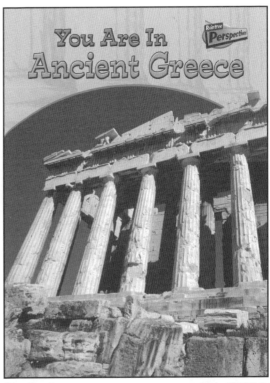

Hardback   1 844 43286 6

Hardback   1 844 43287 4

Hardback   1 844 43288 2

Find out about the other titles in this series on our website www.raintreepublishers.co.uk